The Language of
Paisley

UNIVERSITY LIBRARY

SETON HALL UNIVERSITY
1 8 5 6

Gift Of

Maria Mazziotti Gillan

Poetry Collection

SETON HALL UNIVERSITY

SOUTH ORANGE

NEW JERSEY

The Language
of
Paisley

Deborah Gerrish

Copyright © 2012 by Deborah Gerrish

Library of Congress Control Number:	2012915600
ISBN: Hardcover	978-1-4797-0413-2
Softcover	978-1-4797-0412-5
Ebook	978-1-4797-0414-9

All rights reserved. No part of this book may be reproduced or transmitted in any form or by any means, electronic or mechanical, including photocopying, recording, or by any information storage and retrieval system, without permission in writing from the copyright owner.

This book was printed in the United States of America.

To order additional copies of this book, contact:

Xlibris Corporation
1663 Liberty Drive Suite 200
Bloomington, IN 47403
1-888-795-4274
www.Xlibris.com
Orders@Xlibris.com
116469

*For my husband Jim,
and for the memory of my beloved family*

Acknowledgments

Warmest thanks to Maria Mazziotti Gillan for her unwavering encouragement and support. My heartfelt thanks to Sondra Gash for her poetic wisdom, sense of humor, and whose vision sustained me in the completion of this book. Much gratitude to Laura Boss and Colleen Fletcher for their insightful perspectives. Thanks especially to Michael Smith, Judy Chevelle, and Linda Lederman for guiding me on my writing journey. Many thanks to the Geraldine Dodge Foundation and its program for educators, Clearing the Spring, Tending the Fountain, in promoting the art of poetry, and to all my teachers, peers, students, and for the support of the community of poets.

Grateful acknowledgment is made to the following journals and organizations where poetry will appear, appeared, or earned recognition. Some of the poems previously appeared in the chapbook entitled, *The Language of Rain,* published in 2008.

Adanna, "Putting on Grief"
Ararat, "The Dining Room," "Avon-by-the-Sea," "Portrait," "Winter Solstice, Oak Ledge, New Hampshire," "Holocaust Hauntings"
Bridges, National Endowment of the Arts, The Poetry Center, Passaic County Community College, *"*Grandfather's Funeral*"*
Exit 13, "Harpooning the Tale at Arrowhead," "While Hiking the Shenandoah National Park"
Florida State Poets Association, Inc., "While Hiking the Shenandoah National Park," honorable mention
Goldfinch, "Blackbirds"
*In the Biblical Sense, "*The Call of the World"
*Lips, "*Blackout*"*
Offline, South Mountain Poets, "Thirteen Ways of Looking at a Tennis Ball"
Paterson Literary Review, "Paisley," "Marzipan," "Mother," Editor's Choice, 2006, 2009, 2011 Allen Ginsberg Poetry Awards, The Poetry Center, Passaic County Community College
Paterson Literary Review, "Always," "Reverie"

A Note from the Author

Over twenty years ago, I started writing about my Armenian heritage when I began journaling childhood experiences in a writers' workshop at Rutgers University. My grandparents lived in Diyarbakir, Turkey, until 1914, just prior to the Armenian Genocide. As a result of religious persecution and military pressure, they were forced to migrate, fleeing Turkey where they had resided in an Armenian community for generations. My grandparents traveled to France and then booked passage to the United States. Carrying few personal possessions with them, they entered through Ellis Island and settled in Paterson, New Jersey, known as the silk center of the country at that time. Once there, my grandparents bought an apartment building and established an ethnic food business where they sold everything from imported coffee, olives, figs, meats, pastries, and prepared Armenian delicacies.

Their home was embellished with artistic paisley patterns. As part of my heritage, paisley decorations have always intrigued me. Even throughout adolescence, paisley designs with their bright details and shapes would take my breath away. At the same time, it was subliminally part of my upbringing. There were oriental rugs covering the floors and walls, scarves and shawls my grandmother wore, heavy silk patterned drapes that framed the windows, dresses in gold paisley, and my mother's elegant preference for paisley sweaters, table cloths, and accessories.

For me, this preoccupation with the language of paisley is enigmatic as well as inspiring, and it represents the connections I have to childhood and the development of personal style. It is a bridge, a bond and association with family, a common theme that threads and enriches our heritage. It becomes a symbol that anchors me to past generations and charges that foundation with stability, with familiarity. For me, exotic swirling designs represent the beauty and creative intricacies of existence, and the emotional and inspiring link to others through art, through language, through its suggestion of possibilities. Within this paradox of the paisley print, the pine and flower, one that weaves a set form while at the same time hints at the free form of vivacious creativity, one discovers there exists a sense of constancy through its self-imposed language. It symbolizes order evolving out of the initial disorder of images in the same way art is made. It is comforting for me to know that abiding in this vibrant burst of originality, this contradiction of conforming and soaring, what is of most importance, is that the potential to invent, the potential to discover, lies hidden in the universe of paisley, a source of creative energy to be tapped over a lifetime, over generations.

—Deborah Gerrish

Contents

Grandfather's Funeral *1*
Paisley *3*
Medz Yeghern *4*
Poetry *6*
Avon-by-the-Sea *7*
Marzipan *9*
Always *11*
Portrait *13*
The Dining Room *14*
Winter Solstice, Oak Ledge, New Hampshire *15*
Mother *16*
The Waterloo Rock *17*
The Poet *18*
The Paisley Shawl *20*
Field Notes *22*
While Hiking the Shenandoah National Park *23*
Goldfinches *24*
God's Land *26*
Cicadas *27*
Kiawah Island *28*
Whale-Watching on Cape Cod *29*
Blue Heron *30*
Smitten *31*
Waikiki *33*
Pelicans *34*
Blackbirds *36*
Two Noble Creatures *37*
Ancestors *39*
Holocaust Hauntings *41*
You Listen to the News *42*
Sublime *44*
Griefwork *45*
Memorizing a Poem in the Book While Walking *46*
The White Robe *48*

Pilgrim *50*
Reverie *51*
The Call of the World *53*
Babbling Tongues *54*
Eight Tales in Blue Jeans *56*
Thirteen Ways of Looking at a Tennis Ball *57*
The Teacher Gives Ear to Fifteen Homework Excuses *60*
Early Tennis Following Last Night's Rainfall *62*
The Left Remembers *63*
Winter Moon, Summer Moon *65*
The Smell of Spring *66*
Florence, Italy *68*
Message to Myself *69*
The Poet in Me *70*
When I Grow Up *71*
School Days *72*
Maybe I Am Too Acquainted with Poems *74*
Child Fleeing *76*
Eggs and Bacon *77*
Whimsical Scarecrows in the Berkshires *78*
Rude Cow on the Country Road *80*
The Jackpot *81*
Sarasota Moon *82*
First Words *84*
The Singing Candle *85*
Godspeed *87*
Harpooning the Tale at Arrowhead *88*
Faisant de la Bicyclette *89*
Elegy for Shakespeare *90*
Dream in Verse *91*
Putting on Grief *92*
Blackout *94*
Beyond *98*

Go ahead destroy Armenia. See if you can do it. Send them into the desert without bread or water. Burn their homes and churches. Then see if they will not laugh, sing and pray again. For when two of them meet anywhere in the world, see if they will not create a New Armenia.
—William Saroyan

Grandfather's Funeral
December 1, 1964

I remember I just turned fifteen—
at the hospital
your enlarged stomach,
thick white hair,
radiant face.

The sterile room, its lack of movement,
hushed but for the foreign voice
of the humming oxygen tank
shaking our sky.

Massive heart attack, age 83—
thinking of my grandfather's Bible,
the largest I ever saw resting
on the dresser in his bedroom,
as we all file into the funeral home,
tiny ants dragging regrets behind.

Thinking of his stories, how he ended here—
how he began here in Paterson, 1914,
how he and his bride fled
Diyarbekir, Turkey, that unforgettable July
less than one year before the Armenian Genocide.

Sold all her jewelry,
her heavy gold heart,
his etched timepiece and chain,
her rings. A small offering for passage
for two on the *Oceanic's* last voyage.

They were only teenagers
as they left their family,
fled in a horse and buggy
that steamy summer afternoon.

The screeching parakeets,
the undulating fields of watermelons—
how grandfather's weeping mother
couldn't persuade the young couple to stay,

sent her sons to stop them,
his brothers, Joseph and Abraham
tugging at my grandpa's coattails
screaming, "Don't go, please, don't go,"
chasing them down the dusky road
as they hightailed it to America.

Paisley
Paterson, NJ
1955

My grandfather from Diyarbakir* knows little English.
He always asks me to wear the gold paisley dress
with the purple velvet sash when I come to visit.
On Grove Street, we sit on the silk damask sofa
Aunts Freida, Annahid, mother, and I,
dipping braids of *choreg* in our tea.

Grandfather and the men drink *arak,*
six crystal glasses placed on a silver tray,
mountains of almonds, apricots, Turkish figs.
I can still smell his pungent cigars,
see his rosy face, hear the deep-bellied laugh.

Grandmother scurries in her closet of a kitchen
preparing *dolma,* rolled grape leaves.
In the parlor, Persian rugs covering the floor,
we play backgammon in this castle above the grocery store,
snapping pistachios between our teeth as in the old country.

I grow drowsy with their Armenian chatter,
the phonograph hums exotic music, and
Pretty Bird, grandmother's tiny blue parakeet
brought from the other side,
chirps along from its corner of the kitchen.

*city in Turkey

*Medz Yeghern**
Diyarbekir, Turkey
1915
> Who still talks nowadays of the extermination of the Armenians?
> —Adolf Hitler

1. Gendercide

Diyarbekir fuels March winds
the chasm of hell boils—
generations lost.

Der Voghormia

Men separated from families
as slaves they dig their own graves—
bayoneted, beheaded, hanged.

Women's souls on fire,
death march in Syrian Desert,
girls sleepwalk in seething heat.

Der Voghormia

Mankind in camps
gaunt faces, hopeless,
shadows in the night,

they cannot murder God.

Der Voghormia

2. Mass Tomb

In the Syrian Desert, in the network of caves, lies Armenia, lies skulls, legs, arms, lies burning identity, and when the untouched bones breathe again, when birth comes to the dry bones as it will one day, after ninety something years, they will speak in ashes, in censored pictures, they will speak to the scalded memory of the world stage . . . the bones, the dust will come back to tell, they will chant through the windstorms, their national dirge, their national anthem, in the desert they will cry out, remember me, remember me.

*Medz Yeghern: Armenian phrase that means "the great calamity" referring to the organized killing of 1.5 million Armenians by the Ottoman Turks in 1915
Diyarbekir: a city in Turkey
Der Voghormia: Armenian for "Lord have mercy"

Poetry

Runs through my veins
red rivulets of memory
prayers of the night
wings of the day

Breaks south
to the mouth
in joyful noise

Runs through my veins
pulses north to the eye
then east to the ear
to the tip of the sky.

Avon-by-the-Sea

Remember chewing Wrigley's
in our '55 Oldsmobile
quenching the sugar then
spitting out gum?
Our annual family
vacation at the beach:
When we reach our hotel,
my sisters and I
race to the game room,
the smell of an old
cedar closet airing
its winter memories.
Gold rug and heavy silk drapes
gaily reflect sunlight
that squeezes in.
Pedestal tables are checkered
with red and black boxes.
Some even claim
ivory chess pieces,
others just decks of cards.

Follow the carpet down
the hallway to the TV room where
Ed Sullivan packs a crowd of faces
smiling at the talking mouse.
Run through the empty cocktail lounge
out the front doors beneath the striped
canopy to the vast wooden porch,

where all the grandmas and grandpas
rock in squeaking chairs,
where their chatter
mingles with beach laughter.
The sea the salt the sky,
I take a long breath
of the new air.

Marzipan
Paterson, NJ
1960

Grandma, don't go—
stay with me this night.

Even here, your slight shape,
wire glasses, chiseled chin,
your hair, a twirled bun at the nape,
an apron that smells
of rosewater and almonds.

Even now, you stand at your pantry
chewing gum, offering me
in your thick accent,
a yellow box, the word Chicklets
written in red.

You, who could hardly sign your name in English
on checks, your personalized checkbook,
who wobbled in black trendy heels, unsteady in America
yet copied a silk dress pattern from a Paterson store window,
working your sewing machine at home.

When I come to visit,
I cannot remember you doing anything
but serving and rolling out marzipan
and yes, cooking chicken in the tall copper pot—
sharing your *choreg**, pita, nuts, and apricots.
I take in sounds and smells of your apartment,

even dream of huge barrels of olives
in your grocery below.

   Even now, at the counter top,
   you fashion marzipan into miniature fruit,
   deft fingers folding, shaping, decorating,
   glossy tiny oranges, limes, crescents—
   just yesterday chilled in the icebox,
   now soft, covered with powdered sugar.

What glorious feasts we have at that oblong table
seven of us huddle to break bread and laugh together,
grandfather tells stories in Aramaic which none of us understand,
delicately shaped marzipan sorted on a pedestal dessert plate.
I breathe in eggs, vanilla, the sugar paste of almonds.

You smile a lot and feel at home in your kitchen.
I don't remember seeing you anywhere but there, except at church:
once at a bazaar and then after you took your last breath,
the day you really went home—
the birds sing, overpowering the sermon,
children's voices from the outside
travel through the sanctuary,
the chanting and strong incense,
a confection of who you are,
a confection of the road that leads you here.

   Grandma—
   stay with me this night.

*Armenian biscuit or roll

Always
for Arlene

My sister is
always dancing
my sister is
always dancing
when she visits
she draws me in
like the sea
always smiling
when she visits
we twirl
her in her blue
organza party dress
velvet ribbon
streaming behind
we do cartwheels

she throws off
lace socks
beneath flowing skirts
her crinoline ruffles
she does handstands
headstands
spins on tippy toes
plié and arabesque
takes leaping jumps
whirls across
the greenest grass
her lips are moving

Amazing Grace
How sweet the sound

Joyful Joyful
We adore Thee

my sister is
always dancing
when she visits
in my dreams.

Portrait

These thoughts wash my mind:
Even though they're dead twelve years,
my father's eyes shine,
my mother's mouth curves upward.
These thoughts wash my mind.

The Dining Room

See the old couple at the dining room table
waiting for the doorbell to chime
the old familiar memories like a thousand tongues.
She dozing with her glasses at the end of her nose
as he too nods off then snaps himself awake.
See how he visits the tender eyes
of his two daughters wearing blue paisley,
in the portrait that hangs on the opposite wall,
the third daughter dead seven days.
Look at the sagging spirit of my mother's face
and the dull eyes of my father that yearn
for yesterday when young days sang songs
and even praised the sleeting rain.
See the old couple at the oakwood table,
they are the quarter moon of the wintry soul
that needs the comfort of stars.

Winter Solstice, Oak Ledge, New Hampshire

The painting hangs
on rough bricks
above the fireplace.

This is a pristine farmhouse
nestled in thick snowy woods,
two chimneys smoking,
cat in glazed bedroom window,
light lit in back kitchen.

The adjacent red barn buttoned up
for the night where feathery pines
leave fingerprints across its roof,
cozy to memory's eye.

Barbed wire fence twists in the snow,
limber birches do side bends
from last night's ice storm,
blanketed cold mingles with moonlight.

I walk through the front door,
smell of roasted lamb,
warm air rushes me,
I hear my mother's voice.

Mother

Over the years,
again and again

she walked
from the stove
to the countertop
from the kitchen
to the dining room
to the table

with breakfast bowls or dinner plates,
paper napkins or her best linens—
or with cups of barley soup,
platters of lamb stew, yogurt, and green beans,
sizzling chicken, mushrooms, roasted beef,
or roasted chicken, fried chicken, boiled chicken,
carrot cakes and cupcakes, fruit pies, figs, ice cream,
coffee, milk, soda, tea,

then back again
from the dining room
to the counter
to the refrigerator
to the oven
to the cabinets
to the dishwasher
to the drawers
and back to the table.

I do not know
how many steps
my mother clocked,
but I do remember
I never deserved such grace.

The Waterloo Rock
The Waterloo Poetry Festival

So tell me rock, how long have you been here?
Did you travel the Amazon or Nile?
In what schoolyard did pain wear
lines on your smooth face?
Perhaps the power of quiet waters
gave you your polished gloss.
How did you journey the corners
of time surviving history?

You say, *No, No. For me life's been
entertaining, full of Waterloo metaphors:
Clifton's poem of hips that swivel men like tops,
a moth that moves on hinges in Billy's,
Stern's dancing in the kitchen with his father,
Kunitz living in the layers.*

My resting place is a wooden table,
across from the Big Tent
where poets laureate read
what matters matter,
how time heals scars.

The poets tell me that sometimes
pain even presses them to God.

The Poet

Like the Red-Bellied Woodpecker

tapping trees

                      gathering berries

                                          roosting in cavities

The poet digs deep

hearing the call

                      collecting notes

                                          testing voice

Just like the woodpecker

drumming on limbs

                      singing *chuck, chuck, chuck*

                                          flying low then high

The poet surveys the land

Listens for music

                hums the lines

                                revises, refines

climbs the stars,
clutches the moon.

The Paisley Shawl

That Was Then

when she sat down to write
summoning her Muse to drop in
for a casual visit

listening dozing waiting
for her footsteps

a thought
would find a word,
perhaps a phrase but

          the well was empty
          the glass without wine

nothing would happen

just a blank page
the poet, the silent muse
all huddled around
a dry and barren *escritoire*

and the muse had nothing to say

But This Is Now

whenever she sits down to make a poem
she shakes out her paisley shawl
waters the red lipstick palm
in the corner of the writing room

then through pink binoculars
watches barking blue jays

she waves good morning
to the Canterbury Bluebells
takes a sip of orange tea

Shakespeare her muted tabby
flops atop the vintage desk

to the rhythm of his purr
the poet strokes him

he walks across the computer keys
delicately sniffing the mouse

now it is she who whistles
What a Wonderful World
            the call of the sea plays on the stereo

she wraps her shawl
sinks into the paisley
              universe of the waves.

Field Notes

1. Albino deer dumped in the damp night on Dunkerhook Drive.

2. Content as the dogwood on a winding lane, yet forlorn as a heavy dandelion in the rain.

3. Earth-bound groundhogs long to fly like cardinals.

4. Fox-fur shawl, frowning face, young woman not needing anyone.

5. Unexpected illness, hands hold fast, perspire in the night.

6. Dove bar lies as a fist on the car floor: chocolate stains from yesterday.

7. Worn Bible binding unglued: Your handprints on his life.

8. Zebra bee in begonia, a paisley honey jar.

While Hiking the Shenandoah National Park

> *They reckon ill who leave me out,*
> *When they fly, I am the wings.*
> —Emerson

Ten spotted cows
huddle beneath hemlocks
in the valley of Virginia heat.
I pass them while
hiking the Appalachian Trail,
winding from Maine to Georgia.

Shutting my eyes I see
a Sunday supper in the
empty cabin on the ridge,
taste pecans and raisins.

Climbing higher than rocks
to the mountaintop, I want to fly,
try wings over the valley like a blue jay,
that royal splash in the summer sky,
that watchdog of the forest
who rides heaven on wispy clouds.

Today I fold these dreams,
press them into my journal,
then shake their corners
windward at the winter sky.

Goldfinches
Summit, NJ

As a band of goldfinches
shimmer on the lilac branches

outside the long
Arboretum windows

podium silhouetted

redwing blackbirds
join to socialize

heads tilted
they listen to

parodies and elegies

as they pillage tubes
of pumpkin seeds

feathered cousins
read our lips

our pitches and trills

as we point and chat
during intermission

no critiquing
no red pens

just birds of a feather

and redwings
waiting
for the next reader.

God's Land
Prince Edward Island
Canada

Just another farm
bundled hay,
barley, potatoes
rust brown soil

rural fields
living real
just another farm
where blessings spill
like Irish moss
harvest my thoughts

red earth multiplies
yellow blazing bundles
green royal hills
just another farm.

Cicadas

Like the rush
of migrating birds,
they leave behind
swollen maples
to humble us.

Kiawah Island, South Carolina
February 23, 2011

Take a hairpin turn
past palm trees

where Spanish moss
wraps the Angel Oak

pass the Sassafras Mountains
beyond Kiawah River

where five freckled pheasants
preen on a farmyard wall

where one jumps down
the others fall behind

search for bobolinks
and the Carolina wren

beam at buffleheads and pelicans
relish okra gumbo with yellow bread

in this world
dogs chase cars along the road

run after tailpipes
yelping yah-yup-yah

         then
              fall
                   away.

Whale-Watching on Cape Cod

We boarded standby on the *Dolphin Fleet*
only because fifty-two Russians failed to
appear for the three hour whaling cruise

I'll charge that group anyway the captain stamped
no way I can sell those seats

I remember their buzzing and the electric whiff
of vodka as lightning in the heavy summer air

when the friendly clan appeared, packing us in
we filed down the plank like pods of squirmy fish

talkative blondes bleached small and stocky
brotherly hefty men with hairy chests gold medallions

Russian oohs and aahs as we snapped
like rubber bands from starboard to port side

at the admired humpback flashing its brawny fins
as comrades who sometimes travel alone
but mostly in cliques.

Blue Heron
Longboat Key, Florida

Covered
in a feathered tunic
cowlick stiff
in the tropic breeze

stands like sculpture
on the bisquick sand

waiting

just
behind

the
fisherman.

Smitten

> *Oh swear not by the moon, the inconstant moon . . .*
> —*Romeo and Juliet*

I am one wooed by
the man in the moon
so ideas for poems
come to me whenever
he appears.

Inventing verse
in the glow of his face,
I fill pages in a notebook.

Some earlier poems
turn as ribbons on a typewriter
revolving around town as we drive
across green landscapes,

they wait patiently
on my desk beneath
a mantle of files
sometimes unfinished for days.

They hide in pockets—
change shape during
lockdowns, bomb scares,
reinvent themselves
over a slow lunch.

Up hills near the pond
orbiting the track
to exhaust them.

I realize it is a winding harvest,
but the poems rarely give up,

stand shoulder to shoulder,
no matter how long I howl
at the scratched moon.

Waikiki

Meet me for lunch by the Banyan Tree,
we'll taste ahi-ahi at Dukes,
together gaze at the sea.

Diamond Head and drifting
catamarans quiet my soul,
meet me at three at the Banyan Tree.

Pelicans

1.

In the Gulf of Mexico
two pelicans swing
in tandem across
the gray horizon

like a pair of thieves
they plot their next sting
as cameras flash
on the Spanish Steps

or maybe near newlyweds
at the Trevi Fountain
or outside a boutique
in Torremolinos

they fool their tourist victim
perhaps to steal a Seiko watch.

2.

Pelican wanderers dive
when one misses the bait
the other spears and wins

this all goes on just across from
O'Leary's Tiki Bar in paradise

when the catch slides
they turn circling again

across the open blue sky
with grace, with elegance

in the same way you
set me up to love you
even though you knew
it was a long shot.

Blackbirds

Pass the rhododendron fence on Crest Drive,
gregarious songbirds salute the sky.

Russet leaves fill the nostrils with earth scent,
as gangs of flapping blackbirds swarm and descend.

Even squirrels scurry out of their way—
flocks chug, fly from yard to yard by the thousands.

They move as a powerful train roars down the road,
every yard a new terminal.

Searching the ground for grasshoppers and seeds,
they churr while they burrow freshly fallen heaps.

Intoxicating music, blackbirds, leaves.

Two Noble Creatures

Two noble creatures rise from the forest,
sleek chestnut coats shimmering in August sun.

Their long napping done,
the male deer visit my birdbath
at exactly 4 p.m. each day—
as if seeing the world for the first time.

They commune at this spring,
a woodsy well of youth,
rippling, brisk, gold refreshment—
as two parched children at school
steer toward the fountain.

Much to my consternation
and within seconds,
out of nowhere to be exact,
the trees tremble, the skies blacken.

Battalions of blue jays,
their weedle-weedle resonating,
squirrels skirmishing in the grove,
the squabble of black crows in flight,
rent this placenta of peace.

The two males vie for the first sublime sip,
antlers shine as metallic towers in the sun.
They butt heads, branches of racks crack,
fireworks fly through the forest.

The earth shakes, the sun hides,
the unsteady chalice
sends whitecaps over the edge
to pachysandra below.

The smaller male, like a vanquished schoolboy,
looking pale (if you don't mind my saying)
backs away and waits his turn.

Two noble creatures rise from the forest
the same time every day,
shimmering in the August sun.

Ancestors
for my grandmother Freida

The front row audience of ancestors
applauds her every performance
their deep Armenian eyes follow

from time to time she notices
a raised brow a strong headshake
they are angels prompting her

as she moves forward into the light
she has come further than they ever dreamed
their weathered faces warn where to walk

sometimes their eyes glaze with tears
sometimes they sparkle like morning sun
without a word they speak what matters

housom* carried by survivors
toiling in factories and tailor shops
laboring at silk farms and olive orchards

freedom seekers searching bronze streets
riding the waves of witnesses
they bathe their souls in Jesus

they pass God's torch
one heritage one generation of tongues
speaking and thinking fluently

in one tongue to new generations
great grandmothers great grandfathers
women's women and men's men

all sitting in a row
watching with anticipation
what move she'll make next.

*Armenian word for deep sorrow and sadness

Holocaust Hauntings

Everyone is polite, blotting wet eyes,
viewing proof of the annihilation,
another rape of mankind.

Where photos show empty eyes
unable to comprehend their sorrow,
where hugs could not make
the dark go away.

Hundreds of shoes piled in a heap alongside
hundreds of toothbrushes and razors
piled beside ghosts of tormented Jews,
gypsies, undesirables, the handicapped
echo the shrieks of my tortured Armenians.

Screams never heard across cultures
until fear reached America's steps.
The stench of decaying rubber,
yellow jewels, gold teeth,
the odor of urine and excrement,
still loads the nostrils
with terror.

You Listen to the News

> *Drive, you said, because poets must*
> *bring the news to the next town.*
> —Martin Espada

On the highway from Morristown to Cleveland,
I read poems about peonies, herons, fishing all day—
jot down lines as you attend to national news,
then reflect over more poems and write one of my own.

On the radio, you listen to the report
about a terrorist on the plane
from Amsterdam to Detroit,
how passengers thwart his attempt
to implode himself,
how a hero climbing over seats
puts out the flames,
shackles the nightmare.

Now I read a poem aloud about snowfall,
mountains of winter, memories of the past,
naked sky, gray trees inviting white cover,
a small cottage warm and dazzling—
slumped sofa, calico cat in the window.

You turn the volume up
wanting to hear the President's comments
on the terrorist who tried to *destroy the plane.*

Blizzard outside as we drive north,
against our windshield,
icy flakes scatter in many directions.

Above the rooftops,
chimney smoke tailgates
the falling snow.

He says, *Just 60 more miles to go—*
cars circle us, taillights lift off,
in my mind I'm still back there,
fiery flames spiral into space,
everyone trying to arrive
anywhere in my poem
before nightfall.

Sublime

A good poem
holds the hand
of the reader.

A great poem
holds the hands
of the clock.

Griefwork
for Eve

Thought I was—

not ashamed to say I'm woman
the very bone, flesh of Adam.

But apples multiply
before my eyes

as I slowly chew, the chunky pulp
rolls wisely off my tongue,

sweet juices seep
from the creases of my smile

turned inside out.

Now fig leaves loom
on trees outside the gate,
the royal key no longer fits.

Thought I was—
the apple of Your eye.

Memorizing a Poem in the Book While Walking on the Treadmill

The drone of the treadmill quiets my mind,
I return to the words on the page in the book.

*It is an old story, if it happens
Sometimes now, sometimes never*

I hang on those words—
an old story, maybe now maybe never.

I read the poem again and again.

*Since the woman paces, the report
Since the nurse hesitates, the x-rays
It is an old story if it happens
Sometimes now, sometimes never*

I swing my arms, running, and keep the pace,
bending each word, stretching each phrase
as lines recycle,
one foot in front of the other.

Again, I say the poem.

*Since the woman paces, the report
Since the nurse hesitates, the x-rays
Since the radiologist is quiet, uncertainty*

I am whispering words
singing them, silencing them
then saying them again.

Sounds bump and trade places
an old story if it happens
when it happens
why it happens.

The last lines resonate in my head,
syllables spoken, a halo of words,

Since there is nothing significant, release,
Since there is nothing significant, release.

The White Robe

Here I am
on my knees
again

in the dressing room
of the medical center
hamper in the corner

where each patient
discards her robe
gray rug beneath

on the other side of the wall
the birds are back
the robin has collected
her own brick and mortar
wood chips twigs leaves

as she patiently waits
her fiery breast warms
the newly laid eggs

one day her young
will touch stars
fly in and out of heaven

but here I am
on my knees
again

draped in
blazing white

barely leaning
on the bench

hands raised
in praise

sanctified
beneath the
bluest sky.

Pilgrim

It's an old story
that's often been told

I am a pilgrim
in this land behold

a stranger on way
to the City of Gold

in danger oh Lord
protect my soul

for today I pray
lighten my load

it's an old story
now along I trod

on my way
to the City of God.

Reverie

It's raining in New Hampshire
outside the upstairs bay window
beyond the trees they call to me,
my ancestors.

From behind giant birches,
my sister steps forward in the gray,
her auburn hair curls,
her dress, pink chiffon.

She twirls about
as when she was young,
her soft dark eyes lock mine
as rain mingles with tears.

Mother and Dad follow,
swaying like swans,
dancing and singing to
the Lord of the heavens.

Then the grandmas decked in pearls,
all in black as in the old country,
carry Easter baskets covered
in yellow cellophane.

The skies open, and the rains pound
hard against the window pane.
Their shining faces draw me to the past.

Praise to Thee for bringing me
to these witnesses of ancestors
who have come so far
to this foreign place,
this strange America
where they did not know a soul.

The Call of the World

We were afraid of the night,
the world scratching at our back door

keeping us awake, sleepwalking
creaking floorboards

to investigate restless rooms
turning on lights

transforming our old Victorian
into a jack-o-lantern.

We were terrified at night
when the scratching turned into roaring

we held our ears as the volume increased
shaking our heads from side to side.

We were afraid in the night
but through an upstairs window

saw the world with its neon lights
jewels with discounts slipping away at midnight

Mcmansions with no money down,
cha-chinging one-armed bandits.

As the cool moon looked away
we were paralyzed,

when the doorbell rang,
we did not answer.

Babbling Tongues

As I type at the keyboard
looking out the window
over the top of my PC,

I spot a burly squirrel
sitting on a branch
of russet oak leaves.

Its tail is moving
every which way in
a speech I cannot say.

On a nearby trunk,
another hangs
upside down

tail flat and curling
head to the ground

signaling and speaking
in squirrel tail talk
glued to a limb
beneath a waiting gray hawk.

I am transfixed by
these tail tongues of Babel,*

and bushy flags of victory
waving from oak belfries,

their barrier language fence
over which I have no say.

But what do squirrels know
about possibility?

What do I know
about escape?

*city in Shinar where the building of a tower is held in the Book of Genesis to have been interrupted by the confusion of tongues.

Eight Tales in Blue Jeans
for Hemingway

Napa Valley
        At *French Laundry*, Cabernet tie-dyes jeans

Maui
        Bicycle crash on Haleakala wrecks jeans

Waikiki
        Volcano bicycle tour wearing recycled jeans

Chateau Frontenac
        Strolling the boards in holey jeans

At Woodstock
        Organic music wearing madras jeans

Near Versailles
        French beret, French toast, couture jeans

In Giverny
        Composing poems on noteworthy faded jeans

Le Week-End
        Not my mother's jeans in Paris

Thirteen Ways of Looking at a Tennis Ball

I.

Among twenty royal palms,
the only moving thing
was the fuzz on the tennis ball.

II.

I was of three minds
like the can
in which there are three balls.

III.

The ball soared through the summer air.
It was the core part of the drama.

IV.

You and your partner
are one.
You and your partner and the ball
are one.

V.

I do not know what I love best,
the sound of the ball skipping the tape
or the sound of the ball off the sweet spot.

VI.

The court with thick Har-Tru
is dry as fallen palm fronds.
The ball, rallied back and forth,
imprints the clay.

VII.

Oh parched players of Sarasota,
why do you seek the perfect ball?
The yellow ball you stroke
will lead you where you're going.

VIII.

I know country, classical, hip-hop, and jazz,
the rhythm of the ball, the smashing overhead,
and the crack of the volley.
I also know the ball is engaged in that which I know.

IX.

When the ball flew outside the lines,
it marked the need for us
to win the next deuce.

X.

At the sight of other balls landing on our court
in the middle of a crucial point,
even our opponents let out shrieks.

XI.

She rode along the Palisades
in a roadster convertible.
A nightmare obsessed her, imagining
her chariot, a hopper for practice balls.

XII.

The clouds are shifting.
The ball must be in play.

XIII.

It was daytime all night.
It was drizzling,
and it was going to drizzle.
The ball hung heavy in the sky
just to the right of the hook of the moon.

The Teacher Gives Ear to Fifteen Homework Excuses

1. I did it last night, but I left it home. I'm doing it now.

2. You must have lost it 'cause I put it on your desk this morning.

3. My mom saw it, but I left it at home, really.

4. You didn't write it on the board, and your website was down.

5. Maybe it's in my book bag. (Ten minutes later) It's not there.

6. Honest, my mom put it in the garbage. She said she'll bring it here at 2:45.

7. We got a new printer, but it doesn't work, really.

8. Our parakeet, Sammy . . . he had an accident.

9. There was a soccer game last night, so there was no time.

10. Oops! I did page 27 instead of page 277.

11. My book was left in my desk. When I came back, your classroom door was locked.

12. Someone stole my book bag this morning. They took my spelling and all my other homework.

13. All my homework is in my notebook, my notebook's in my book bag, and my book bag is in my room behind the computer table.

14. I left all my books and homework in my dad's car. I need a pass to call my mom.

15. Homework? What homework?

Early Tennis Following Last Night's Rainfall

It is early morning, and
the moss green clubhouse

sits unpretentious

the sun stops
near the path framed
with oversized planters
blue hydrangeas

                         jays call from thick trees
                         I lunge for a short volley

speckled butterflies swerve
across our court, distracting me

dark clay freshly brushed
the tug of cut grass in the air

I need to abandon my drop shot

                         I must give up over-trying

in my corner of *Eden.*

The Left Remembers

In the evening,
she practices her ritual.

The right hand fastens rollers in her hair,
the left hand carries the clips.

The right paints nails with polish,
the left hand blots the cuticles.

The right hand removes the lipstick,
the left watches how it's done.

The right massages hand cream,
the left leans back and sighs.

In the morning, sunrise emboldens the room
as she sits down to write a poem.

The left remembers while
the right takes notes in margins.

The right hand types the scribbles,
while the left hits arrow back.

Then later, the left invents the lines,
while the right hand types in words.

The left lifts a cup of coffee,
the right prints out final copy.

Long after the sun is a streak
in the summer sky,

and painted stars shine
in the glossy night,

southpaw eclipses the right.

Winter Moon, Summer Moon

Snow sparks behind spooked
long-legged galloping deer,
whites out chestnut flash.

The ivory-tailed doe
dances across the gravel path,
hind legs fly into the warm thicket.

The Smell of Spring

It seems it's always spring
when you sit down
to write a poem—
so scrape the woodwork
swab the floor and ceiling

clear the clutter
of computer and notebooks
piles of pens clips
metaphors that need undoing

the lists of verbs
and flipped clichés
clear even your family tree
from your drafting table

then arise and open
the winding windows
cleanse the dull air
allow a gust
to surprise your lungs

cast a warm eye
on the casement porthole
where spent sunflowers
lean on a rickety fence

where schoolchildren
throw cubed snowballs
at parked cars

where the chipmunk
is flattened in the road
by one reckless act

where our indoor cat
vanishes into
the screen door

then drift through the gate
of jacaranda trees
the smell of spring

notice small bullet ferns
a smoky sky of sachet
the maker of the moon

listen in the dimly lit garden
for the flute of the wood thrush
praising Him beyond glorious.

Florence, Italy

God's gateway to paradise

    where the cypress towers
        above pink oleander

    where silvery olive trees
        of the Apennines

    and figs and cedars soak
        in the sun near umbrella pine

    where sunflowers dot
        the countryside like needlepoint

    where craftsmen of the Lord
        paint His Gospel on walls

His book of living reasons

        Firenze

Message to Myself

Poet,

be faithful

to your gift

or

                          it will slide

                                            as a jewelfish

lost

                        in the mind's

deep.

The Poet in Me
Botanical Gardens
Montreal, Canada

Sings of monochromatic
rose gardens

brushes Canadian bluegrass
with the language of touch

rises to lemon geranium
blue cardinal flower

        words cascading like
            the bonsai set in jade

lingers near lily pads where madame
sketches peonies on sacred canvas

swims with speckled carp
surfing emerald stones

sips chrysanthemum tea
in Chinese gardens

decries hemlock white snakeroot
red baneberry and moonseed

exalts the purple foxglove
bending fountain grass
       then climbs into tulip tree houses
           plucking petals

this poet in me seeks to loose
the poet in me.

When I Grow Up

When I grow up,
I want to be a poem
that tweaks the soul,
humors funny bones.

I want to sing
about living deep,
breathe on men and women
when I grow up.

School Days
Whittier Elementary School
1950s

I cannot forget the Bible on Miss Parentini's desk in her 6th grade public school classroom. Each morning, she walked down the rows and called on someone to read Psalm 1, Psalm 100, or the 23rd Psalm as part of morning exercises.

First we read from the Bible, recited the Pledge of Allegiance, everyone participated, everyone saluted. Classmates stood tall next to chairs pushed into wooden desks with tops that flipped up, each one with a small hole carved out where an ink bottle snuggly fit.

My home room teacher was stylish with dark smooth hair, a thick shiny chignon coiled dramatically, thin gold rimmed glasses, knew my sisters, made me comfortable. Larry sat in the first seat in the front row, fidgeting, Barbara sat to my right, chattering until the moon rose.

Lunchtime was different back then, we could invite a teacher home for a long lunch. I remember when my 3rd grade teacher, Mrs. Martin, came to my house at noon, flashy tulips were blooming, and I looked upon everything with wonder, including her.

On this day, clear as spring water, she walked home with me, mom greeted us at the door, our mini dachshund barked hello, too. On the patio, there was a vase of lilacs, and the glass table was lavishly set for three of us. We ate salad with oranges, chilled green Jell-o

and sandwiches on warm Italian bakery bread. For dessert, mother skipped the chocolate Hostess Cupcakes, which she talked me out of, presenting instead grandma's moist paklava, cut in diamond shapes, thick with walnuts and drizzled with homemade syrup.

Mrs. Martin wore colorful glasses, had light brown hair, which she pulled back tight in a band. She wore a feminine yellow shirtdress with a flared skirt, belted to show off her slim waist, sent a paisley note card of thanks with her flowery signature at the bottom.

Mr. Brien led the best social studies 5th grade classes teaching us to do-si-do and square dance in a room without desks, swing our partners, shuffle our feet, bend, crouch, ham it up to the lively music. *No kissing Seven Up games allowed on school property,* he would say.

My hall of fame teachers were all unforgettable, and I think of them often, but I will always remember 6th grade. How could you have ever known, Miss Parentini, that because of you, I would remember those psalms, recite them in a classroom 50 years later at a Dodge poetry

workshop when asked to retell a memorized poem, song rhyme, or remembrance learned as a child. As we go around the table and it is my turn, most of the 21st century teachers in the room look at me incredulously when I tell them how

once upon a time, in New Jersey public schools, for morning exercises, students were chosen alphabetically each day to read songs from Old Testament scripture about God and how he delivers his people.

Maybe I Am Too Acquainted with Poems
> *It is what exists between the lines.*
> —Ferlinghetti

Maybe I put too much faith in the love of poetry,
thinking that poems are my friends
when they never admonish me if a line
is clunky or a phrase is wrong—
nor support me if I run out of money
to send them off to journals.

Maybe I put too much faith in the sounds of poetry,
thinking poems are fathers, mothers
humming as they fold towels, change the oil,
brew tea, show me who I am.

But why would I imagine that Frost
could give personal advice on the miles
I need to cover in the 21st century—
and even unravel unknowns about
boundaries and fences, ice and fire?

Nor is it clear what lies beyond the split road,
and what to do if both paths appear grassy.
Nor why would I dream of swinging on birches
thrown into the arms of heaven then earth
unless I too believed *earth is the best place for love*?

Maybe I put too much faith in poems as comrades,
borrowing their sweaters, coats, shoes,
sharing pomegranates, apples, figs—
even taking long walks together
along the river, thinking that
iron really sharpens iron.

But what about those other poems
that spill nature, written by a recluse
confined to her New England, her small bedroom.
She whispers Death and Heaven in caps—
tells it all at an angle, even the light is slant.

Maybe I rely too much on poems—
maybe I am one too acquainted while
memorizing and dreaming them
as I sleep against a sun sometimes
blank though in itself.

Yet I shall arise and sit at the computer,
continue to record notes over time
as a violinist playing sheet music,
composing another group of friends.

Child Fleeing

The child sitting across from me
in the shoe department
slides off her chair and screams
that she wants to leave as she
tugs on her red balloon. *The innocent*

*and the beautiful have no enemy
but time*, said Yeats, but what
about this child, so completely
in her own world

wearing the little ballet slippers,
jeweled toes, which glitter in
the light, and which she throws off
as she rushes to the escalator,
fleeing her mother
on bare anointed feet.

Eggs and Bacon

Our cat Paisley
wakes us this morning
5 a.m.

she plays ping-pong
with the curtain cord

her muscle memory
is as keen as the sun

her game of choice
determines what time
her trophy is served.

Whimsical Scarecrows in the Berkshires

> *Art comes to you proposing frankly to give nothing but the highest quality to your moments as they pass.*
> —Walter Pater

Walking in the wide field,
I dream we could play scarecrows
covered in Salvation Army clothes

you could be a man
in wooly trousers
madras shirt
suspenders

I could be a woman
in paisley skirts
chiffon scarf
fluttering in the wind

our wired ribcages
stuffed with hay
our beeswax faces

or we could be artists
dressing each differently
some in the garden
some raking
some dancing

nearby a pond
another teaches
a child to fish

or you the banker
in a pin-striped suit
briefcase in hand

flying to catch the next train
leg in air
felt hat swooping.

Rude Cow on the Country Road

Near a pasture
of jolly green
with milk white
picket fence

rests a house
adorned
by apple trees,

trees that trim
a pond spilling
with catfish.

Nearby
cartoonish cows
with tender eyes

blink flies away
that cover their
patchwork skin.

Moo, Jacob calls
to the one that
moves close.

With casual grace
she flashes a look
turns her back to him,

leaves a puddle
in reply.

The Jackpot

1.
On the cold sidewalk,
Johnny plays jacks and wins again—
pennies.

2.
Thirty years later,
coins like stars vanish overnight—
dust.

3.
When the sun appears,
no matter what state you are in—
gold.

Sarasota Moon

I.

Shroudedin striped clouds,

tonight the curious feline

moon

transfixes from

the ledge of the sky and

burnishes

a path on the

Gulf

where

waves

like cornrows of noisy mice

race

from sea to sand.

II.

Late at night, I look out the balcony

                        overlooking the tide

my cell phone is ringing

in a daze, I grab the TV remote and press—

    the moon grows louder   the mice run faster.

First Words

My daughter points to the moon and says cookie.
—Marie Howe

The child,
captivated
by the moon,

takes small bites,
names it cookie.

Within
seconds,
the night

disappears,

and moondust

leaves a footpath
of crumbs
on the worn carpet.

The Singing Candle

On her 44th birthday
he surprised her

with sunflowers
Chanel 5

he took out
the lemon cake

hid in the
coat closet

set it down

on the glass
dining table

one bright candle

lit up the
snow frosting

inside the candle
a music box

whistled alone
make a wish—

in the early morning
the buttery fists of the flowers
were soaked in perfume

but please, do not be concerned,
last year the cake ran off
with the gold heart.

Godspeed
for Shakespeare, the Cat

Just after he burrows
the mattress for an eternity
front paws digging

just as he hums his cat lines
nesting beneath the comforter
in a fetal curl

just then he decides it's time to leave
creeps off the bed backwards
turns and nods farewell with his tail.

*Harpooning the Tale at Arrowhead**

Rain pours out the north window
Melville sits dreaming

the giant white
Leviathan hauled in

eyes fixed on whaling
Greylock Mountain

his finger follows its outline
tracing the enormous hump

copies of *Typee* on the bookshelf
of his unfurnished study
Billy Budd not yet bloomed

aye thar she blows

he aims his barbed spear
at the apparition

striking
the tale
he wants
to tell

fountainhead
harpooneer
at his pine desk
a restless vessel.

*Herman Melville's home in The Berkshires

Faisant de la Bicyclette Sur La Plage
Prince Edward Island, Canada

pump lean
pump lean
red sand
blue sky

pump lean
pump lean
moon snail
white pine

pump lean
pump lean
sweet flag
damselfly

pump lean
pump lean
lighthouse
willets cry

Elegy for Shakespeare
July 4, 2009

We buried you
in the backyard
beneath the elm

A shrine to
your seven lives
their ashes dust

I walk to the house
shovel and spade
weigh me down

Breaking my heart
your green eyes still peer
from fresh soil—

*Don't forget
where I live,*
you say.

Dream in Verse

> *A poet: someone who is never satisfied*
> *with saying one thing at a time.*
> —Roethke

It's 3:36 p.m. on Thursday, played tennis, showered, grabbed a bowl of soup, sipped an iced tea. Smitten with magnolias and the early smell of spring this March 21, thinking about writing the perfect poem as I drive to a workshop about writing the perfect poem.

Trying not to let it slide, as the missed dream I failed to record this morning in the notebook on my night table, barely remembered white flashes, faded faces, red smudge, awakened without a picture, left without a story, a comet spinning in space. But I know how much I fall in love

with types of poems, the sonnet, prose verse, and elegy, how I rehearse the poet doing more than one thing at a time, a triolet kidnapped by its own form allows haiku to move in, a thief behind the wheel. The longer I live, the more I realize poetry is nothing more than dream charged with

color: a short-lived trill of the wood thrush, the setting Sarasota sun, a seamless Halston dress, flowing Dior, gray noise of the city, St. Patrick's chimes, mulberry trees, olive, and vineyards—before they disappear.

The longer I live the more I realize the longer I write, life is dream in verse that vanishes behind clouds as the afternoon sun, forgotten with the last fallen petal of the magnolia, shriveled yet captured by the wind.

Putting on Grief

I've put on grief—
know what it's like
to skip meals
lose memory
walk into walls

I've put on grief
as a one-hundred-
year-old dress hidden
in a back closet

Borrowed from ancestors
my mother, aunts, grandmothers,
great grandmothers

Torn with stains
a dreary faded gown
outlined in shadows
with dropped hem
and missing buttons

I've put on grief—
a costume too large
for this invisible body
afraid its design
will unravel me
as tumbleweed

Wanting to move
on to another place
but not yet ready
to escape this
curse of sorrow

where with threadbare soul
I am sentenced to hollow
rooms to wait it out—

I beat my chest,
shred my clothes.

Blackout

> *What thou lovest well is thy true heritage.*
> —Ezra Pound

Tonight
I feel like I am living
through World War II—

it is pitch dark
in the neighborhood,
and the sound of sirens
pierces the Bitter night.

I cannot see past my toes,
and the street lamps
have forgotten their
call to duty,

there is a town curfew
so no creatures venture out
aimlessly to see what goes

so I hide in my bedroom
beneath the covers,
shades blackened and pulled tight,
vanilla battery operated candles
light the Gloom so I can
at least write a poem.

It is endearing, writing poetry
by candlelight, even if it is battery run,
the flicker of the wick
and the shadows on the walls
place me in the late 19th century,
scribbling as Emily did in the Deathly Dark—

hints of warm wax permeate the Air
ink like perfume
silk feather Pen transports
to another dimension

causing me to forget
the Heavy trees
downing nests of wires
droning generators with
their acrid fumes
that disturb my sleep
water grenades that
bounce off the roof
clank down gutters
to the broken earth

causing me to wish
I am somewhere else
until the night
whispers a new Vision.

But what about Irene Opdyke,
a Christian holocaust survivor,
who hid a dozen Jewish victims
in the basement of the villa
where she worked,
the home of a Nazi officer.

How she played Wagner on the victrola
to conceal their weeping,
how she told those closest to her,
*We must pretend to be German
so we can be Polish again.*

Oh, how we pine for normalcy
when it is taken from us,
how we long for the Ordinary
evening walk, cutting cucumbers,
running hot bath water—

have you ever thought
what Music you will play
when your life swings
like a tooth on a string?

Tonight, another Irene, the hurricane
the whirling winds like bombers
the cracking thunder that heightens the sky
floods my basement then the second floor

floating curtains, pictures in frames, refrigerator,
chairs, coffee cups, plates, embroidered pillows,
lamps, waterlogged plants, a surreal scene
covered in an oily veil

whirling winds like bombers
cracking thunder that breaks the sky
on this moonless night of the year—
storms that ravage the soul's Soul.

What poetry will you write
when Calamity rushes
your walls in Desolation,
when locusts cover
and strip your land?

Who will you turn to
when the universe conspires,
when the earth falls away,
and the rumbling of the sea
invades your one Sacred life?

Beyond

> *For now we see through a glass, darkly:*
> *but then face to face . . .*
> —I Corinthians 13:12

It is here where the towering
buttonwoods shade the great lawn,
the kindly mint breeze mingles
with sea air sifting memories

to a time of lemonade porches,
grandmas in squeaky rocking chairs
that echo laughing seagulls
above distant waves.

Thinking back to
sun-drenched summer days
when ocean air was as pure as linen,
I recall green days aglow
as young blades of grass.

Mesmerized by the choppy sea,
I dream of who I am,
what I will be,
somewhere between
earthdust and angeldust.

I glimpse the whole dream,
that I could catch up to who
I am and not be so far behind
that which I am becoming,
a vision that never ends.

Sitting in the warm sand
where musings carry me away,

I gaze the way dreamers do
as the sun leads my thoughts

farther than the mossy jetty,
farther than fishing boats
spilling with their catch.

Seeing past sun-bronzed faces,
schools of diving dolphins,
a horizon of cruising cormorants,
I dream beyond generations of stars,
beyond the paisley moon.

About the Author

Deborah Gerrish is the author of the chapbook, *The Language of Rain.* She is an award-winning poet whose poems have appeared in *The Paterson Literary Review, Lips, Adanna, Ararat,* and *Exit 13*, among others, as well as various anthologies. In 2003, she received an Edward Fry Fellowship for scholarship and accomplishment as a doctoral student at Rutgers University and received her Ed.D. in Literacy Education in 2004. She taught in the New Jersey public schools for over thirty years as an English teacher on the secondary school level. She and her husband reside in northern New Jersey, where she teaches writing.